Love Letters
to Him

*Inspiring intimate relationships
with God*

52 reflective poems and essays

Sheila Ford

LOVE LETTERS TO HIM

All Scripture taken from the Holy Bible, NEW INTERNATIONAL
VERSION®. Copyright © 1973, 1978, 1984 International Bible Society. All
rights reserved throughout the world. Used by permission of International
Bible Society.

International Standard Book Number 978-0-578-03358-7

Library of Congress Cataloging-in-Publication Data
Printed in the United States of America

Content

LOVE LETTERS TO HIM

Acknowledgements

God, I love you.

Introduction

52 reflective poems and essays

I hunger to be fulfilled and desire to be loved. Love Letters is speaking love the universal language to the world and breaking the silence of the church.

"Longing to be Loved"
Intense, strong, and spiritually passionate are the words that describe Love Letters to Him. This year long book of poems and essays explore intimacy and sexuality in our faith. Love Letters has been called a 21st Century Song of Solomon expressing climatic emotional highs to agonizing painful lows.

Love Letters a conversation between the Bridegroom *(Jesus)* and His Bride *(the Church)*. It's sure to satisfy so many that have been starving to experience the Author of Love in a renewed way. These letters are changing the way women
discover their identity, relational expectations and desire to be treasured.

These challenging and stunning poems unfold in hopes of transforming the way women allow themselves to "Be Loved." This genuine love affair explores four themes or aspects in the relationship. This includes the Courtship, Honeymoon, Marriage and Conversations. These themes reflect the powerful way Christ may transcend the dysfunction of human sexuality with the anticipation of a deep and intimately spiritual bond with His Bride.

The compilation of these letters allows the reader to not only listen but begin to participate in a holy conversation only experienced through the miracle of trust, hope and faith. *Love Letters to Him* is passionate, stimulating and biblically based. These letters are poised for single or married women. Each "letter" challenges the reader with personal reflection to ponder life application for spiritual growth and personal accountability.

These poems and essays can be read all at once or in a mode of weekly reflection and application.

<u>Literary Themes</u>

The Courtship
The Honeymoon
The Marriage
The Conversations

~~~

Reflection questions
Application & Accountability
Please consider the questions
provided or create your
own.
Appendix

Author's Notes...

I believe it is very important to note how deep and probing this material can become. Depending on your life circumstances and experiences this could be painful as you uncover old wounds or offenses. What is exciting about this discovery is the freedom so many say are on the other side of facing your fears.

Here are a few things to consider in your discovery:

- Everyone is different. Give yourself permission to scratch or dig underneath the surface as you reflect and prepare for freedom and healing in this process.

- When disclosing your heart make sure it is in a safe and confidential environment.

- If you don't have trusted or spiritual friends get help from a professional Counselor or Therapist.

- Some insurance plans and/or community agencies offer free or reduced fees for counseling support.

- Don't let **ANYTHING** stop you from becoming free and uncovering your next **"whole self."**

Understanding His Love through "The Courtship"

The beginning stages of a courtship are that of testing or trial and error. The relationship is often a dance of determining a match, do you fit together and will this relationship work? In our courtship with Christ we face difficult experiences that often move us to ask a series of questions. Why are you letting this happen to me? What did I do to deserve this type of treatment? I thought you loved me?

If you've never experienced a courtship with Christ this is an opportunity to explore the potential of a more meaningful relationship with Him.

It's during these times we have the opportunity to embrace a love that can penetrate our disappointment and failure and move us to trust the relationship as we embark upon a greater level of intimacy and passion. This section will address how to see God's love at work in your challenges and increase our faith for His purpose in our lives.

Understanding His Love through "The Honeymoon"

The Honeymoon typically is hot, passionate and highly personal. It is a time that lovers are free and uninhibited to express themselves romantically. They are constantly looking for opportunities to serve, prefer and observe their lover. This section reveals the fervent love God has for His Bride, His pursuit for her and His desire to penetrate her being for His glory. This section invites the reader to go beyond their limited physical expressions of love and perceive an immeasurable and unfathomable entree to His character about His adoration and infinite grace in their relationship.

LOVE LETTERS TO HIM

Understanding His Love through "The Marriage"

Often people use the word love so loosely. Love in marriage has lost its value, credibility and enchanting interest. These letters examine love with commitment, confidence and courage to stand and stay despite great challenges and temptations. God's love through marriage is unmovable, unimaginable and unconditional. This kind of love can only come from God because God is love.

These poems and essays unwrap the reality that impact our emotions and the maturity needed to weather life's difficulties. This section reveals the level of growth and ripeness that comes in trusting God because you know He is and His love covers every aspect of our lives.

Understanding His Love through "The Conversations"

These letters are an array of topics ranging from homosexuality, addiction to racial and gender disparities. The conversation pours out the cries of the Bride and in some cases His response to her pain. These letters while controversial also position themselves for intriguing dialogue and action if stimulated.

The Courtship

Week 1 - You're in my dream
by Sheila Ford

Not one waking moment do I not see you as evidence
Your predetermined plan in me you've taken full residence
Choices I make daily I see
The fruit of what you told me to believe

I can't sleep I wake 2:00 am or 3
How can I fulfill tell me would you please
All that I thought contrary to the promise
Falters in my hand goes away in the distance

Sometimes it feels like a nightmare or curse
Nothing materializing the last to be first
Realizing purpose yet seemingly aloof
You do not lie your promises all truth

I push past my doubt I see it within reach
I block all the naysayers their relationship a breach
There are signs I am inclined to trust you even more
You shut that place removed that space only one open door

I move rest trusting your best steady it all seems
Now you're not **in** but you **are** my every dream

LOVE LETTERS TO HIM

Week 2 - He stole something from me
by Sheila Ford

It was a typical weekend. Our family was visiting and my mom was making my favorite baked beans and potato salad to go along with my dad's ribs I loved the combination of those flavors. All the kids were in my little brother's room. I was the oldest so the responsibility of keeping everyone in line always came back to me. "Sheila why didn't you stop him from doing that?" or "Sheila you're the oldest you know better…

I still don't remember why we weren't outside but I believe we were on our way. As we headed toward the bedroom door my family member turns around and grabs my breast. Shocked, I push him back and told him to stop. He laughs and runs out ahead of me. I stood there stunned thinking he touched me, I feel naked. When I went outside I felt as if he could see them. I couldn't concentrate. Without notice he came from behind and pushed me to the ground. His hands were everywhere, on my bottom then between my legs.

I got up and punched him with all my strength, but to no effect. His laughter sent chills through me. I ran in to tell his mother, she brushed it off as "rough housing." "Kids being kids" she said. I looked at my mom with an earnest plea. They called him in and he denied everything.

This behavior went on for some time. It became customary during their visits. I was nervous, had no peace and he'd frequently catch me off guard and grope me again. This ritual elevated to an irritation on the part of our parents as I try to fend off my aggressor with futile results.

Once the kids spent the night and he was suppose to sleep with me. His sibling was going to sleep with my brother. The bunk beds seemed miles apart and my parents room a world away. My fear is mounting. I could feel his anticipation. He'd have me just where he wanted me. My plea to sleep in the living room was dashed – to the bed without lip service I was told.

I laid there quiet and still. I could feel his breath. Every moment my heart beat faster. My hands protected my chest but my bottom was exposed. I lay awake hoping he would sleep. Then he struck, his hand on my rear. I hollered out, elbowed him in retaliation and ran to plead my case with my parents.

My father had taken all he could. He asked the boy in courtesy but shortly cut him off. It was late, well past midnight. My mother called his parents. Before I knew it my dad was driving them home and he never spent another night at our house.

He stole something from me.
I didn't feel safe.
My family didn't seem to believe me.
I didn't feel strong.
His laughter belittled my worth.

My family members didn't know they changed my life forever. Even as I write this my reflection of the events are clear, but the impact has become dull.

Abuse of every kind has a way of whittling away at you. It's so subtle. It made me second guess my value, my tolerance and my strength to overcome.

I've wondered why the experience happened. Even asked why did God allow it, then thanked Him for protection from something even worse.

Week 3 - Her name was Rosanne
by Sheila Ford

Inappropriate touch I didn't yet I did
The sun hot but my temperament frigid
She was older aggressive more the same
I wanted a friend she'd remembered my name

The other kids I could hear them playing
Wondering what we were doing then impatiently waiting
We were open view seemingly no one could see
It felt awkward I wondered what would be

I did not like it I told her to stop
She was looking for a special place to hide a spot
There was danger anx my heart beat
I couldn't seem to move or shuffle my feet

Why didn't I tell I wanted a friend
Could I explain it was hard to defend
She was older mature pretended it was a test
My solace was I never had undressed

Someone to see I needed a favor
Obliged by an onlooker it was our neighbor
He promised to disclose the dirt he'd uncovered
Intently to find the path to my mother

Relieved and perplexed mixed emotions unaware
Sexuality protected by His Hand and His care

Week 4 - I said "No!"
by Sheila Ford

His unshaven stubble scratched my face and his breath smelled like stale beer. My arms were pinned and I couldn't move. He's so strong. My mind was racing. How did I let this happen? My brain now flooded with a list of questions in an instant. His hand moved up my thigh reaching for the button on my pants.

College life was filled with a wave of new and exciting changes and challenges. One of which was the reality of purchasing text books. They were so expensive. Seventy-eight dollars?! I can't spend that on "one book!!?" "Miss" the clerk exclaimed, "do you want the book or not?" I was asked to step aside until my decision was definitive.

I must have had the look of young and inexperienced underclassmen on my forehead. As I considered my options of limited resources over the next two weeks, another student – in his third year approaches me to discuss my dilemma. He says "you can get the same book used for less than half the price." I knew he was lying and thought it was a pick up line.

He insists and gets others to convince me this was a customary practice on campus. "$20.00" he said. I asked, "why would you sell the book for so cheap?" He said, "I don't need it anymore and that's what people do." I quickly agreed, hoping others hearing our conversation wouldn't steal my deal.

He told me the book was in a room over the campus sandwich shop. That was the hangout for all the students. Everyone went there and they had the best hot dogs in walking distance.

While pinned down I quickly recalled growing up and a having a family member frequently touching me inappropriately. During that time my anger grew and so did my strength. I learned to fight and preventing him from permanent violation. I was saved that time.

I've always been strong and smart. How did I let myself get in this position? Why did I believe him when he said the book was at the top of the stairs? Why didn't I question his motives? It appeared to happen faster than my sanity. He was friendly, well known and seemingly harmless.

It was dinner time and I could hear the roar of students below. They might as well have been a thousand miles away. No one could hear me. I asked again "where's the book?", as he sits on the bed. Then it happened in an instance. He pulled the book out of the drawer and grabbed me simultaneously. In one swift motion I was thrown to the bed.

His mouth covered mine. I couldn't speak. It wouldn't have mattered, the noise below was much too loud. I couldn't think or believe what was happening. As his hand moved over my button, quickly loosed I become scared. My emotions began to race. I considered my limited choices. I began to pray. God please help me!

Amazingly I recall a self defense show that discussed remaining calm if ever attacked by a rapist. So I did. The class taught the psychology behind the mind of a rapist and their lack of defense or loss of control when their victim is compliant. So, I started to kiss him back.

Shocked by my reaction he stopped his aggression for a moment. I asked him "why are you rushing? I told him I thought he was attractive and asked if he had anything to drink before proceeding." The look on his face was disbelief and he quickly jumped up and said he didn't have anything but a guy down the hall did. He left the room in haste. I grabbed my book, collected myself on the way out passing the cheers of the sandwich shop and headed straight to the campus police.

The police chastised me and explained my charges would most likely be dismissed claiming his word against mine. In addition I willingly went to his room and there was no physical evidence of a struggle or abuse.

I cannot tell you the anguish, anger and shame I felt. I had been violated and there was nothing I could do about it.

Once I calmed myself I began to recall the series of events that early evening. It struck me so strong – God heard my prayer. Desperate, short and simple…God help me! He did. He saved me from my aggressor and once again protected me from further abuse.

It was in that instance…another moment where and how my life was changed. I experienced the Hand of God personally and relevant. I saw Him at work for me. He was my protector and my prayers deepened that night. They were of great gratitude and increased wisdom as I grew and knew Him as my closest friend.

Week 5 - Eye Candy
by Sheila Ford

They have my name they say it's a treat
Shaped and prepared for the male eye to meet
Delicious to the eye calling me candy
Wanting to paw hold and hand me

Drooling hoping salivating to get a lick
All for a cheap thrill arousing their stick
Sweet to eat they say wondering how I am
The more they want influence me to glam

This cycle is degrading bitter at the center
I can't get out alone I'll seek out a mentor
To turn this around and show me a new way
Forever putting off I must start with it today

Someone said I'd be an apple of His eye
Effortless yes I won't even have to try
To make an appealing case for a surface dessert
When we both could have more building up the bigger Church

We are a body I'm a part of a plan
Creating kingdom interest not possible with natural man
Change your eye the window for the soul
Repair the breach in gender Healer make us whole

Week 6 - Hold Me
by Sheila Ford

I'm cold I'm hot my emotions unsettled -
  Who will see and understand my pain
  Does anyone care I think I'm insane

I'm unsettled confused my spirit is mature -
  Released and complete my life bursts with joy
  I'm tested and requested not to be toyed

I'm a see saw amusement park converging at best -
  His design for me seeking growth and dignity
  I'm held and kept contained for all eternity

Week 7 - Gay or straight
by Sheila Ford

I want to hold you your sexuality
Remove those devises penetrate your identity

Lay you down help you remember
My love not tough but oh so tender

I'm sorry about what he did how she stole
Your innocence and made you cold

Insensitive to who you really are
Abandoning each relationship making them afar

Do you see me trust me to make you a virgin
I'll start with your heart and repair like a surgeon

Healing those wounds those you don't even know
Removing the scab it won't even show

Except that I was there at the middle center
Stage of your come back to me if you venture

I feel your pain go on and cry it's alright
I'll hold you and love you and make this my fight

Block out the noise learn to hear my voice
I'll show you what to do how to make your choice

Pick me first love me best
Intercourse you can't imagine try me a test

LOVE LETTERS TO HIM

Week 8 - Don't you want me
by Sheila Ford

Don't you see me trying your attention
I'm interesting didn't I mention
My weight not the number I'm going for you see
The battle ongoing I don't know what to believe

My lumps and bumps the mirror doesn't lie
I hate to look yes even my thighs
My skin has paint injected in some cases
Seemingly not happy no matter what the races

My teeth are so white as ivory snow
I'm matching entertainers it's all for the show
I can't afford the clothes I wear and hair
Why won't designers make affordable it's not fair

I wish he would talk to me listen to my thoughts
Appears he can't get past the surface what's not bought
I can change the world would he just look up
Focused on the superficial only concerned with my cup

My eyes are the window to my soul
Gaze in intently you soon could mold
A friend daughter wife leader
If you thought with your heart and not with your peter

I'm healthier now changing what I show
Knowing not what you believe but what I grow to know

Week 9 - My hair
by Sheila Ford

Too long too short too thin around the edge
A focus of my attention becomes a major hedge
Too dark too light the textures not right
Can't go out like this I wish it were night

Too coarse too fine I need some extension
Expand my exposure increase my attention
The hair mine known each strand He counts
Not measured by what but by an internal amount

Growth pressing through surface moving in the Son
Creating an understanding new life has begun
My ends being trimmed cutting away what's not good
Some chopping also needed as if I were wood

My hair like a crown observed by most
My spirit seen in another world judge by the Holy Most
What do I want expect people to see
Desire to refocus and inch and degree

Cut it off start a fresh I need a genesis
Determined to fight against my growth the nemesis
I see a style hairdo it started with a cut
Reaching past the follicle searching for the rut

LOVE LETTERS TO HIM

Week 10 - Circle of gold
by Sheila Ford

The circle of gold to most called a ring
In all actuality it's really a thing

Many of us single covet wanting it so
People looking at my hand and automatically know

I'm alone without formal companion
No one to say they'd take my hand in

It looks so pretty some simple and dull
Sometimes I want to cry overflowin and full

So much pressure and all this attention
Don't want any to say or even start to mention

The fact that I don't have this label or handle
Increasing my anx with every new candle

Gold is a mineral refined in purification
It should be esteemed rather those hatin

I want to be free from the pull I feel in the ring
Not that I don't have it but without it I could sing

Sing and express my ability to know
Purification is needed for more than just gold

Week 11 - My past lover
by Sheila Ford

My past lover what could have I been thinking
Hope of a fairy tale or something I'd been drinking

What'd I see why think it would last
The ripple of each one's lives brings present the past

What were they to me even if only one
No place space could ever be like the one with the Son

Emotions fly high heat only for some moments
Scene fixed for me to groan in

Brief pleasures pass if that at most what did I get
Gave up more once feet hit floor some memories make me sick

Why regurgitate or reflect what's the reason or the purpose
Present now wanting how to remove it from the surface

A smell a tone a look caught off guard suddenly
Distracting my mind confusing focus subliminally

Why did I tell this why do you listen I hope that you do
Tell your sisters daughters babies son let them all start a new

Make up your mind determine to find true passion at the start
Relate to Him start within and no one will steal your heart

LOVE LETTERS TO HIM

Week 12 - A Woman or a girl
by Sheila Ford

Are you a woman or a girl
Does man's action rock your world

Will you stand or will you lay
Allowing their decision to delay

Your purpose focus is it controlled
By degrees status or opinions sold

Are you sure you know who you are
Or caught on the path to be their star

Can you decide or is your opinion shaped
By what she said that made you ache

Are you a baby in diapers needing to be changed
Has the world warped your thinking need to arrange

Are you mature enough to know where you're going
Staying the path compassionate still flowing

Are you woman enough to hold out for soul mate
Or are you settling appeasing the quick fix date

Have you past puberty deflating emotional fluff
Has the woman in you said enough is enough

Stand up little girl see where you stand
The Bridegroom needs production looking for wo-man

Week 13 - He's pursuing me
by Sheila Ford

He watches how I walk
He loves to hear me talk
He follows me and is above
He looked ahead to give His Son Love

He leaves clues to remind me it's Him
I feel guilty when I fall into sin
He sends others to tell me what He said
He makes me laugh cry is this in my head

I thought I saw Him in the way something happened
I needed a miracle no one else could take action
I tossed and turned into the night
My sleep would not come right

He's speaking in so many ways
I tried to run but I wanted to stay
He sees right through me knows me well
He's protecting from pain anxiety and hell

I looked up and He was all over me
Caught by surprise why didn't I see
His persistent pursuit deliberate at best
I accept His pursuing and now enjoy my rest

Reference Psalm 127:2

The Honeymoon

Week 14 - A desire of a heart
by Sheila Ford

A desire of a heart beats pumps for me
It starts as a dream then reality
What am I looking for what do I see
A glimpse of my success in love dwelling and free
I wanted I hope for speaking things that are not
Touching an unimaginable place owning a new spot
It is it can it's willingness to be
It starts as a dream then reality

I feel my life engulfed in a flower
No thorns or thistle fresh dew of a rain shower
Did you see me feel me touch me in that place
I know it's confirmed and written on your face
I choose to move advance with life directed
Speaking spitting word atmosphere infected
Contagiously blessed through all eternity
It starts as a dream then reality

You feel me hear me calling your name
Your ocean washes over me just as it came
A desire of a heart beats truth for me
Undeniable indescribable willed in Him to be

Week 15 - Intimacy
by Sheila Ford

Intimacy…He's in to me see, never felt like this before
Attentive to every detail opening my doors

Listening intently patiently does He wait
Early with the sunrise never is He late

He knows what I need when I want attention
Appeasing sometime but requires growth did I mention

He told me I'm beautiful intelligent in my heart
Affirming what I'd hope to be confirming from the start

He likes what I like cause I like what He desires
We finish each others sentences I write He inspires

He's here with me I can see even when I don't
Think He notices all I need missed promises He won't

He makes love to me that's His will but there's so much more
His way His smile His attributes I can't tell you how I adore

What's great to me how I can see what matters to Him most
That I lay down in me He's found His glory that I will boast.

Week 16 - His smile
by Sheila Ford

I can hardly imagine life without
Drawing my attention as I go about

I see it in His eyes He watches my walk
I hear it His voice He speaks I'm taught

My day is brighter just when I think
My load a lot light because He won't blink

I get excited when He calls my name
I'm special to Him yet He knows you the same

He loves and cherishes me I see it in His smile
I trust patiently the wait only for a while

Week 17 - Let Me love you
by Sheila Ford

I want to hold you stroke your hair
Let you let go of life casting all your care

On Me because I can handle this
Amazing capacity I'm there and in your midst

I saw what you carried then giving away only a portion
You're confused on how to handle it's all a distortion

I love you in the way you are accepting what you lay
I love you in what you didn't know that way another day

I love you when you hurt because I cry too
I love to make you laugh cause joy you'll soon pursue

I want to hold you supporting your back
Teach and help you manage all of what you lack

I see relationships increasing life's stress
Some for your pruning some for your test

I see where you're alone you don't have to be
Isolated from my agents they're there for you to see

I love, will protect cherish you with all my heart
I love you with uncontainable love your mind can't even start

I love you more than you can think imagine or comprehend
Protector guider lover closer than any friend

Week 18 - I need to hear your Voice
by Sheila Ford

I waited for you it appeared an eternity
Impatiently as such in a state of maternity
Unable to explain the state of this experience
Listening for signs your tone not apparent

The weight of this pressing in on me
What I just felt what could that be
New development and growth in me in the making
Protecting from the enemy his wanting he's staking

I look to the hills my help from above
Longing to know hear you where is your love
The weight enlarging purpose greater to bear
Your answer quite ambiguous movement do I dare

I want out I want off move me off the table
Let's abort and pretend this only a fable
You see me in agony merciful says your Word
Just one is all I need a promise to be heard

I'm your sheep I know it remembering from a child
Water breaking mention this that what and how
There it is still and soft I heard it over fear
Voice banish all iniquity Word knowledge is all I hear

Week 19 - Kiss me
by Sheila Ford

I hurt today no one seemed to care
The pressure of life I desperately tried to bear
I needed your hand to lay on my hair
To stroke my place needed only you were aware

I cried today no one seemed to know
The tracks of my tears only your eyes would show
I wanted you to hold me never let me go
Abandon my resistance never telling you no

Kiss me in those places only you can touch
Tenderize my temperament creating so much
More of your likeness sweetness as such
You see me destined to be purposed enough

I feel your breath upon my face
Kissing each tear with your grace
Even now you will erase
Tracks of my pain by your embrace

LOVE LETTERS TO HIM

Week 20 - A Longing
by Sheila Ford

I long to see your face
I will see it with your name on my forehead

I long to hear your voice
I will hear it powerful and full of majesty

I long to feel and to touch
One touch from you old things become new

I long to engage in embrace
My breasts to you like clusters on the vine

I long you lay me down
You allow me to rest in the peace of you

I long you kiss my lips
Your lips are better than choice wine

I long you feel my hair
Humbly I use each strand to wipe your feet

I long to hear your heart
My ear attentively pressed against your breast

I long for intimate discourse
Overwhelmed to hear how you feel me

I long to be one with you
I live for you dying for your return

Reference: Rev 22:14, Psalm 29:4, Matt 14:36, Song 7:8, Ps 23:2, Song 1:2, John 11:2 Psalm 69:32, Song chap 7, Phil 1:21

Week 21 - A Virgin
by Sheila Ford

I feel how you feel scared of the night
The air in the room so tense almost sight
You've felt me before warming up to you
Progressively you're guarding down barriers become few

Your apprehension is your constant reflection
The ones that held you used you then you felt rejection
You should of never let them touch you like that
There was no commitment depth did it lack

Your acceptance not to stand then to lay
Down with deceptive promises never once obeyed
I'm pulling back the covers exposing your secret
Revealing your tenderness seeing your neglect

Of the spot that needs to be covered hovered with attention
Going deep within subconsciousness completing new
dimension
I know you never felt like this before
I found a sweet place opened hidden door

Did you know I could keep you and let you know
Fondle your intellect emotions in privacy we grow

I want to erase the impurities from the past
Make you mine today forever will we last
Keeping you for myself never letting you go
My virgin preserved in a precious Holy glow

Week 22 - My Chambers
by Sheila Ford

It's quiet here no hustle or busy sounds
We're not rushed or distracted no one else around
I waited all day just to see you greet me
Your attentiveness apparent what will we achieve

I hear your voice it's sweet when I read
I love when you direct show me and you lead
Erect is your way knowing what you know
Submission of myself embrace as I grow

What is that I hear a song
It's our favorite now I remember it from so long
It reminds me of when when we first met
How you courted drew never to let

Me get ahead of your plan for a purposeful way
Intentional by design each step preparing for today
Each hour seeming a day oh how you made we wait
Standing on the threshold of each promise you make

This time with you I'm reminded of another thought
The day you forgave me for everything before and after He
bought

My life was changed in one single moment
The veil removed receiving with atonement
It's all made a fresh in chambers privately agree
My love unconditional just give you to Me

LOVE LETTERS TO HIM

Week 23 - Lay me down
by Sheila Ford

You start with a glance emerging throughout the day
Your words a sweet way I'm leaning want to lay
You helped me showed me what I needed most
Counsel and support you never had to boast

Dinner so surprising a treat so glad that you offered
I needed to rest you knew my heart made softer
Our bed framed with love and patience supported by passion
Your hand a guide come inside before you take an action

You lay me down I want to lay feel the comfort of your peace
Your presence known what you've sown from the crown to my feet

I think on you want to move with your delight
I feel your hand joy young is the night
Your touch so tender today speaking without a word
The hands talk a language only the inner man has heard

You penetrate all my fears drive out what is wrong
Comfort floods my soul felt power you are strong
I want to come closer deeper let me reside
Hold and change me you see all I cannot hide

You start with a glance a bid to you to find
Laid down so sweet pleasure completely my rest in you divine

Week 24 - Your Hand
by Sheila Ford

Where do you search moving to find
The secret of my conscience I'm ready unwind
I feel your intent indent in that place
I move with you new level new space

Your hand is firm deliberate in placement
Gentle and soft others past I begin to resent
You know me find me ask me without words
I answer sweetly response you've already heard

Oh I love the way always seem to know
My makeup intent what I need to grow
Would you release me only to mold again
I see where you're taking me challenged in sin

Your hand is hot testing against its surface
Demanding results all for life purpose
Your hand is cool calming the elements of my night
When I feel you what's wrong is right

Your hand is tender used to discern
The passion of my lifestyle constantly I learn
Your hand is mine left by the Spirit
Directing my feet right what I cherish

Your hand is yours to use as you please
Under your guide I move as you lead

Week 25 - Open Wide
by Sheila Ford

Ah say it spread yourself under the sky
Engulfed in a passionate love affair He touches the inner thigh
Climatic intent momentous increase He fashions
His Hand purposeful finger finds your passion

You're moving intently less resistant do we find
Resting in the elatedness joy you'll find and climb
You're coming now free without hesitation
Overwhelmed and succumbed by Spirit penetration
You open wide say come inside you welcome right in
Spirit saturated your lust demolishing every sin

You are there inside open wanting no end
Indescribable impact inner man apprehends

Let it go let Him know your preference His desire
The passions hot you're in the spot your willingness inspires
Willing to be open to see, life's submission is what's required

*Note; hand on the thigh represents an oath ref; Gen 24:2, 9,
47:29*

Week 26 - Come Passion
by Sheila Ford

I feel you pressed against my being
I start to enjoy the pressure of your leading

I'm coming now can you feel it
The pressure to deliver I decide and submit

Passion intensifies trusting where you move me
Intentional design I admit it soothes and agree

Don't stop change is what I need
Passionate resolve I commit and concede

I burn with fire coming running for Him
Changed by the Spirit what now bright once dim

Hot for service igniting new flame
Used by choice kingdom focus is my claim

Do you want to lay down change you in a moment
It's evident the facts are still a proponent

Embrace what He has is laying upon you
It flows yes and soft just like morning dew

Week 27 - Wash Over My Soul
by Sheila Ford

Wash over my soul make it complete
My head down my back thru the toes of my feet

You cleanse me tingle I want you there
Navigating crevices I was not aware

Did you see that that sin it was not of you
I held it for ages death was overdue

Let's go deeper find a hidden place
Searching unproductive thought only you can erase

Water by the Spirit gentle or rushing damn
Wash over my soul creator great I Am

Deliver, comforter, healer in one space
Universal, eternal, infernal omnipresent by your grace

My soul needs a refreshing fill me even more
Change my heart oh God open another door

Fresh rhema new manna I accept what you feed today
I listen and feel your presence in each and every way

Wash over my soul fresh power to reveal
Transformed by your greatness never to be concealed

Wash over my soul make it complete
It starts at my heart and ends at your feet

Week 28 - My Body
by Sheila Ford

My Bride…

My lips…part speaking truth boldly in the day
My ears…hearing the lies of the world discerning for the way
My eyes…spiritually sharp a dove singleness of purpose
My neck…poised positioned strong bones under the surface
My breast…appealing full of milk ready to distribute
My back…strong ready for battle resolute
My womb…producing spirit one after another
My egg…fertile ready for release by her mother
My hands…reach out compassion for the world
My legs…supporting the weight she's a woman not a girl
My feet…run to apprehend what lips will raise
My face…shines in labor with power and praise

My whore…

Her lips…wrapped around the organ of capitalism
Her ears…plugged truth in hope of appease religious ism's
Her eyes…dim lusting after the ways of man
Her neck…surrounded by a controlling hand
Her breast…dried hard unable to produce sustenance
Her back…bent in submission to false promises
Her womb…barren and diseased
Her eggs…lost their release
Her hands…closed in fear loss of compassion
Her legs…open to deception
Her feet…still and maimed
Her face…hiding behind her shame

The Marriage

Week 29 - I see You everywhere I look
by Sheila Ford

I woke up this morning wrapped around me as usual
      Your love didn't care how I looked or didn't feel
      You embraced me sweetly from my head to my heel

I looked in the mirror I saw you there staring back at me
      You looked average at first then my inner man speaks
      I listened attentively you fill in where I'm weak

I reached for a pot of coffee my hand older than before
It reminded me of my writing experience now even more

My meal so nutritious I'm more mature today. Thankful for its
      Blessings considering your mercies and those without
      I rejoice and want to shout

I prepare to work and see your hand in that.
      Gifted to accomplish purpose you open doors
      Through trials and hopeless nights you redeemed time
                           now it pours

I walk I breathe you're evident all around
Birds weigh on trees wind in the snap of the ground

I love the water and yes I see you there
Your countenance in my reflection you wave at me with care

I rest again and dream of my life I see you in the wonder
My sleep is sweet your hope so deep vision never put asunder

Week 30 - My Feet
by Sheila Ford

My feet are shod with the preparation of peace
Running advancing knowing life is truly within reach
Where are you going can you see the prize
Efficient to cleanse stamina on the rise

Condition yourself you must press harder
Begin with your mind it will advance where you charter
Course is set move where He leads
Your path purposed surely to succeed

What do you know wisdom the coins of your treasure
Each inch you advance a mile by Christ' measure
Cherish the track building muscle strengthen bone
Faith by day increase hope and trust is where you roam

The heel is hard balancing your stride
The balls conform comfort for the ride
Each toe grips its destiny pulling for the journey
Moving swiftly toward outreach kingdom gain eternity

Run the race the prize within reach
Your life is a model run and you teach
Prepare the way vision with His plan
Trust the finish line in His arms you will stand

Week 31 - Who I am
by Sheila Ford

I am your Queen
I stand erect proud and strong
There's no confusion of where I belong

I am your Bride
Stunning flawless magnificent to watch
Anticipate our chambers anx is what I fought

I am your Lover
Knowing only your touch gentle and sweet
You lay me down preparing for our meet

I am your Warrior
Skilled in battle fierce under pressure
Designed for combat built in character

I am your Angel
Mission and purpose available where I am
Dispensing love and grace like a beach of sand

I am what you need
The earth full of your glory watch me model
Understanding now my life not throttled

Week 32 - My Two Husbands
by Sheila Ford

My My husband was on another business trip. They had come more frequently over the past year or so. I had missed him but I had figured out ways to make the time work for me. I'd become very accustom to these long stints.

I was a little nervous. I knew what to wear "that" outfit. I took a shower prepping to look my best. Yes….and my favorite Victoria Secret bath spray…Midnight Moon. It's so fresh and clean. I'm going to wear my hair up – it's pretty like that *(I thought to myself)* What else - my nails, teeth and just a little make up… check, check and check. Ok, now the setting. The room needed to have a feel. The candles I bought last week would set the mood just right. I'll put my favorite instrumental CD in and just let it play in the background. I could hardly wait.

But it was the waiting that seemed to warm me up to Him even more. There was this tension between the anticipation and the anx. I felt the anticipation of what to expect; what would He say, how long would He stay and would He come again? Then the anxiety of what if He decides not to come or what if I don't do this right?

I've never done anything like this before. But I loved Him and well… actually more than my husband. I realized it awhile back and finally gave in one night to His embrace.

He's so sweet, His touch so tender. When He speaks it's always a whisper and when He saids my name, I melt. His intimacy cannot be described. Once I tried to tell my girlfriend, but no words explained the way He makes me feel.

Honestly, I started feeling guilty about six months ago. My husband asked me, if I missed him and I said "well kinda?" He said "WHAT?!" I replied yes…yes of course I missed you. *(that wasn't a whole lie)*

It was just that there was something special about my time with Him. He's always showing me things and taking me places. When we're alone He strokes me in the place that I'm weak and directs me when I feel lost. He holds me close and promises to protect me against all my fears. He's my Father, my Friend and my Comforter. And I'm His Beloved. He showed me where He writes about me in His book. He said I'm the apple of His eye.

His Presence overtakes me and I don't want Him to let me go. All that matters is Him. I want more and find myself working new ways to get back to His place. I have found a treasure and He's all mine! Matt 13:43-45

I've been married to Him since I was a little girl, but wasn't mature enough to handle our relationship. He even told me that what I'm sharing may be tough for some to handle. But I just can't keep this to myself.

His name is Jesus. And His person of the Holy Spirit lives in me and overtakes me when I submit. It grieves Him when I am rushed and it hurts Him when I want to create intimacy in inappropriate places. He respects me and I'm learning how to respect Him more each day.

He's always with me and soon He will take me away forever. But in the meantime, I'm swept away to experience His presence. His love penetrates my heart, mind and soul. The beautiful thing about our relationship is…He teaches me how to love my other husband. After I'm in His presence I'm kinder, more patient, I give and I listen. There is a lot less of me in the way of our growth and I see him with unconditional eyes.

This season of times with Him was ordained. My earthly husband's travel schedule is about to end. But our spiritual journey is just beginning. It was all for our benefit. My Spiritual husband is jealous when I get my priorities confused. And He has taught me well. I've learned to hold my earthly husband with His strength. Our embrace is a tri-cord dipped in the oil of His grace. It is holy and sanctified in the expectation of eternity.

I love you I love you let me count My ways
You are incense in My nostrils My word protect your days,
I desire to hold you and lay you on My breast
Let My heart beat sweetly to reveal details of My test,
You feel Me, receive Me - lives coincide
Our marriage create offspring waiting your womb inside,
Indwell in Me, propel to be
That no man is a deterrent of your promised destiny

Prayer:
Father, thank you for the sweet gift of your Spirit. I cannot praise you enough for the embrace of your love. Saturate me with your presence. I desire you today. May my life be evidence I have been with you and let my marriage be a

witness of your decision and provision of one flesh in covenant
in the earth.   In Jesus' name, Amen.

Week 33 - May 3
By Sheila Ford

Five three grace me fill me with your presence
Holy Spirit, Father Son three in one essence
You are mine I am yours we stand to face the world
What does it mean how can it seem an evil is hurled

He's moving by His Spirit seeing what to take
Uncapitalistic man this content to forsake
Hope in it won't you spit out what constipates
A constant flow to move and grow holding it you ache

Look to me can't you see point out where it hurts
It's underneath your pain and grief look to natural man earth
I am high I look low seeking my child that's a man
Intent to be like river planted tree fruitful in the land

Grow by the Son stretch out pollinate and bear
I'm pruning you stripping you down I know you are aware
Fruitful multiply giving birth for the season
Obedience righteousness move it is my reason

What I planted only I can pluck full of worry no need
It's my season I own them allow me to proceed
Full bloom take your hand off move from the path of my wrath
I am God I error not trust me for what will last

Diamond rubies, minerals will pass you thru eternity will stay

Waiting to see humble to be Spirit the scale will weigh
It is I I Am God God alone I am the great I Am
My statutes law providence in the land will forever stand

Week 34 - You love me….love me not
by Sheila Ford

You love me love me not why it appears a game
Your time with me our relationship not the same
I ask a question ignoring me not an answer or reply
Intentional deliberate at best why would you deny

You say you love me your letter to me you say
You died for me changing world in you no other way
Calling my name I heard you toying with my emotions
I changed for you my life with true devotion

Why did you leave me standing all alone
You wouldn't seed once planted now starting its grown
I'm stronger appears when you're here strength for my journey
Not alone there's your presence trusting you as attorney

I feel your hand we take the stand advocate for me
I know your love from above I'm not guilty but set free
Not alone not denied not a case have you lost
Your love for me there indeed provided at no cost

How'd you know who to show evidence for my case
You changed the time providence divine in every place
You love me love there is no not
My understanding comes in I don't know the plot

Week 35 - Cr'eye's that lie within sin
by Sheila Ford

What can wash away my sin
Who can hold me deep within
It's a battle that rage with great effect
An inner hidden place the natural cannot detect

Who can make me whole again
Jesus seems to unattend
Don't you want me I'm your child
Vessel breaking under weight of life trials
A subtle foe you do not know
Waiting in secret your defenses low
What does he seek, patiently find
Vulnerable unresolve, a crevice of the mind

No other friend I know
Who can make me white as snow
I want to be clean, I want to be whole
Free from within battling for my soul
I cannot hide nor can I sleep
I embrace temptation death wish to keep

Born into sin no hand to hold
My world were crib bars I was cold
I want to be touched want to be hold
The embrace of comfort this life was not choose

Where is my father a motherless child
A desirous woman a bed waiting to defile
Who can long for how long can she wait

A little baby cries out oh' her heart aches
Who will hold her pick her up
She looks to man to fulfill and sup

She hears her name she opens wide
Her heart fulfilled she will not die
Spiritual honor her weight scaled divine
The tempter wage forsaken, her Father's gift in kind

The lie and sin target at fetus
Washed clean and made whole by bought blood Jesus

Week 36 - The Morning After
by Sheila Ford

Let not your heart be troubled doubled full of pain
What you think you've lost is surely for your gain
You hurt you think your agony coincide
I'm dwelling there too let me hold you and abide

Wish not think not be not but who you are
An apple a remnant a beacon seen from afar
You are precious a gem a beautiful delight
This your morning after let go of your night

Do you want what I have do you want what you need
A scarf and cloak of honor what I offer what I feed
My daughter my son separate yet the same
You hear me clearly and yes I call your name

Embrace me love me let me love you back
You'll see no error in my plan nothing will you lack
Mountains I erect valleys I cut low rivers and streams
From time there was time my word has its being

It matters where you hurt I made every emotion
I've seen what you've turned it is sign of true devotion
Don't be dismayed or concern yourself with the matter
What I have in store is prepared in the latter

Latter days latter days fondle not the care of time
You'll look up to see my timing is divine
I trust you my daughter my son more than you imagine
It's trusting me you will see your fate is in my passion

Week 37 - Catch my tear
by Sheila Ford

It was a blur. His mouth was moving but I can't begin to tell you what he was saying. As I moved in and out of attentiveness I kept thinking why? It really didn't make much sense to me. This is the second time and I've done all the right things to prevent this.

As my husband intently listens to the doctor. "Mrs. Ford, I'm sorry but you've had an ectopic pregnancy." I wish doctors would use words we understand. "Ectopic….what's that exactly I asked?" It's when the fetus is found outside the womb or typically in the fallopian tube. My mind was racing!! Well just move it into the right area. With all this modern technology…why can't you? One egg in one womb, is that asking too much?

Growing up I remember watching the Brady Bunch, Partridge Family and the Waltons. I always wanted a large family. But at age 38 it was highly unlikely.

Disappointment is a real dangerous thing. If not caught, I think it can parallel a river water rushing over rocks. There is this subtle yet steady erosion of your faith. It's beneath the surface and no one even knows its happening.

As I lay in the hospital bed I could feel a tear roll down the side of my face then slip into my ear. My husband turned away from me in hopes I wouldn't see him cry. I didn't want to see the hospital counselor. I counsel people all the time, I already knew what they were going to say - they could save it!

Ok, I don't know if you've ever had an internal battle going on inside of you, but it is agonizing. Part of me wants to be depressed and sad and the other part is trying to think of scriptures and the goodness of the Lord. I had a right to grieve...but I also wanted to accept my lot. *(I also have a Type A personality)* Unable to sleep, thanks to the frequent interruptions of the wonderful nursing staff, I laid and I prayed.

I wish I could describe what I felt. The best natural analogy would be to liken it to a huge electric blanket. But it was on top and inside me. I was overwhelmed. I felt God's presence all over me. I sensed Him saying...I am your comforter. Then I thought, yeah a comforter, that's what this feels like. It was in that moment I knew I would be alright. I was in the palm of His hand. I wasn't in denial, I still felt sad that I had lost my baby, but... something was different. I just knew my Father would never leave me.

There is something amazing about God's love. This, along with my large "faith file" has affirmed His provisional support at every point of need. When I'm sick He's my Healer, when I'm lonely He's my Friend and when I am sad He's my Comforter. I love Him and am so thankful He hears me when I call.

As I look back on these years, I smile and think about the one prayer I prayed and thought He never answered. "One egg in one womb." Hmmm...He actually went one step further. My ministry was birthed and He's produced countless spiritual babies by turning my wound into a womb.

Prayer;
Father thank you for the bottle that catches all my tears. Help me to trust you with every aspect of my life. Allow me to accept your grace and mercy in my afflictions. Strengthen me when I am weak and remind me of your faithfulness when my faith fails. I praise you as my comforter and exalt you as my peace. Thank you for turning pain into passion, my tears into testimonies and my disappointment into destiny. Amen.

Week 38 - Tomorrow or Today
by Sheila Ford

Tomorrow is not promised He said focus today
My tendency to look to see what is the way
My heart is heavy not knowing what to do
I ponder thoughts perplexed considering what is true

I feel you with my inner man wrestling with the matter
The dream and course inside begins to flatter
When did you do this where are we going
You hide your answer conceal any showing

How do I discipline the roaming of my mind
Determined to help you access the plan that we find
You know all won't let me fall why won't you tell
The waiting anticipating can have comparison to hell

I'm growing some creating one stronger inner man
Treating myself as enemy to the development of your plan
Today is here what's the notion nothing else resounds
Resolved to trust His word truth I've found

Today is peace letting release all else to go
My heart and mind a fixed you'll see me and will know
It's evident now He's shown me how holding in today
Tomorrow not yesterday spent today my only way

Week 39 - Bring me more
   by Sheila Ford

More opportunity to let you know
More chance to serve and show
More of you to live and be
More more love of Christ to see

More desert to be aware
More patience to know you care
More suffering to grow me up
More tolerance to fill my cup

More mountains for strength stamina
More appreciation when you feed manna
More valleys to see as opportunity
More grace to know there I find maturity

More peace to stand trust that you know
More making of me pruning to grow
More joy at last because I define
More more of you your ways divine

Week 40 - Lasting Love
by Sheila Ford

Lasting Love
From Above
Trying time
Love divine

Giving hope
Let's elope
Leave today
Don't delay

Hoping trusting
Endless lusting
Washed away
Doesn't stay

Feeling free
Wanting be
Held by
Can't deny

His embrace
Seeing face
Lasting love
One above

He's Amen
Begin again

LOVE LETTERS TO HIM

Week 41 - You're coming back
by Sheila Ford

You're coming back I see you on the wall
It was promised well before the fall
Atmosphere unsteady proving liquid signs
Delivering foretelling heaven's by design

Your word changes not what does the world see
Excused phenomena is what it must be
Many called few chosen selected for the work
It takes His hand all through His determined effort

Many called few chosen liquid turns into ice
The Church waxed cold no oil in dead of night
I'm coming back turn the light on see me now
Confront the undesirable I will show you how

You are able trusting me with your life
You are purposed to fight expect opposed strife
Join me warn them let it be known
Each seed you plant much fruitfulness is sown

You are my daughter son purposeful character
It's you who it wants dwell not in the exterior
Abstract may it seem see it in the spiritual
I'm coming back its written on your wall

Written on your heart trusting you to read
You were called and you were chosen sacrificed indeed

Conversations

Week 42 - Abortion
by Sheila Ford

The table is cold it's steel and hard
My mind in pain no one in charge
It's dirty and dingy faces are hiding
Comfort from the reception for the cash I'm providing

It will be over quick nothing will be the matter
The little heart beats it won't be in the latter
I'm so alone the table cold and hard
My senses mask life that could be from afar

It's a secret discreetness none can ever know
How I choose selfishness over what's to grow
The anguish the guilt when will it go away
Wondering her face what it would look like today

The past is over can't erase what is done
Desperately looking for His comfort from the Son
Some say He'd forgive me others damn me to Hell
I want to believe directing my foe to expel

Only choices isolated no hand near or far
Just a cold table it's steel and oh so hard

Week 43 - The Other Woman
by Sheila Ford

Just look at me what can I see reflection
The mirror keeps lying I keep hearing rejection
She's there on his lap his hand around her waist
He can't get enough his love for the taste

He takes another he wants her again
I try to speak don't know where to begin
What did I do nothing it appears
I'm dying on the inside facing all my fears

She holds him soothes him never to let him go
I was promised power and authority do I need to grow
Where do I go seemingly caught in a prison
Life death changes His promise because He's risen

Torn about abandoning the fight she can have him
Having faith in God knowing deliverance over sin
It is a journey not for the faint of heart
It starts at the end knowing the outcome before you depart

Winning victories is what you hear over the chatter
Knowledge she is from the enemy your stand is what will
matter
Laugh and rejoice she is a fool to challenge the inner man
Defeated foe laid at your feet strong and erect you stand

Week 44 - Intimidate
   by Sheila Ford

What is it about you that makes me so scared
The way you carry your weight face how you wear your hair
I look at you you look at me scanning head to toe
Assessing in an instant all you need to know
Did I ask you a question did you give me an answer
You kept your distance from me as if I had cancer

I'm looking toward you wanting to see
A model of what I really want to be

You seem to have a life normal to most
You'd say it's challenged nothing to boast
You know where you're going seeming on the run
Not knowing the weight responsibilities a ton
What's not apparent or on the surface
Is the pain I wear behind my purpose

Emotions can control an outcome if not careful
Management in faith only when prayerful

What you see is not always what you get
Search for the candle within see how bright it's lit
Don't you judge a book by its cover
The one in the mirror could truly be another
Face to pray for agree if not you, don't hate
Recognize the wall might be what intimidates

Week 45 - Dear Daddy,

What does it mean to be called wo-man? I'm pulled and poised, beaten and toyed. Who would be my fan? Misunderstood by most, characterized by toast, who would show my worth in this earth?

My tear stained bed and unstroked head an empty hole to fill. I'm caramelized honey to rich deep chocolate noir. It's evident my life was spent left in the change of my cost.

Do you see me hear me, I'm calling your name. High on life's numbness this becomes my claim to fame. Crack pipe, red light or Entertainment tonight I'm all the same pain.

Will you see me, I exist, am I that great of a threat? Your inability to view yourself is what you are to confess.

I look outward tired of isolation. Found in wrong places attuned to pain. Strength and courage are my legs my hands compassion and love.

~~~~~~

Embrace me if I let you, trust you if you earn
I'd rather stand alone than compromise allow my passion to
burn.
What does it mean to be me wo-man chocolate and delight
Ask my face hear the answer to cut you like a knife

Sincerely hurting,

From your daughters
Written by Sheila Ford

LOVE LETTERS TO HIM

Week 46 - The skin I'm in
by Sheila Ford

Black white brown or hues of beige
Measured by a pallet vague yet weighed
Quickly assessed with the blink of an eye
Did you once stop to go deeper would you try
To see the creation begun in me
I have purpose and destiny

We're probably related possibly the same blood
Linked spiritually same Father from above
This subtle contempt or devalue if less
Confused about true measure actually I'm the best
My life to make a difference in the present and the future
Your look opinion tries to castrate or neuter

The belief and trust of who I am
The joy I'm to feel for how I stand
Look past my skin I see past yours
Forgiving your error daily a chore

The systems created to judge us today
We can demolish if we follow the way
The Truth is we belong to Him the Life begins
With agreement sin is judging the skin we're in

Week 47 - Celebrating Life
by Sheila Ford

My celebration of life its purpose in full bloom
Once permanent tracks now seemingly vague wounds
How or where did we intersect to be
Your impact was sprinkled into my life's journey
Through seasons, times often distant days
Our times become purposeful then they fade

What or how is man measured how does each life account
I sense it's by what we treasure hidden in a limitless fount

From lost children to lost dreams
An appearance of life separate at the seams
What do we search what will we find
More death to carnality revealing true signs
We don't need, want or even like this life
But further desire to desire more of like Christ

A forty and a five only relevant to one
My wilderness and His grace presented then done
The waiting is over surprised to see a latter day
I embrace what's for me joy replaced my decay

You too can rejoice and celebrate with me
The volume of new life if you chose to be
What stops purpose, promises unfulfilled
The deceiver exploits you – you have not sealed

What or how is wo-man measured
Surely not by its hope or what he treasures

Christ' faith is by a perceived belief standard
His potential fulfilled in humble grandeur
For my birthday April 10, 2009

Week 48 - he doesn't love you
by Sheila Ford

Does he know your name
Call you just the same
Hold on to you in the middle of the night
Even when you're wrong or fight

Does he know who you are
Casts your faults all afar
Trusting you beyond measure
Seeing your life as a treasure

Does he listen when you cry
Hold your back dry your eyes
Soothe your mind when insane
Take your loss provide you gain

Does he know you are the best
Not comparable to the rest
Will he take you as his bride
Or make promises until his rise

he doesn't love you like I can
he can't help he's only man
Realize limitations both your audacity
I'm God love unlimited capacity

Week 49 - Straight or gay
by Sheila Ford

Give me your heart straight or gay
Revealing my will when your sexuality lays
A land full of confusion indecisive they say
Straight or gay the controversy weighs heavy today

Born this way or created with a culture
You make my decision held captive we torture
Many opinions about life choices what I do
Lost consideration drunkard slander gluttony over food

What are the facts both think they are right
Caught in gray matter who is wrong black or white
The focus and attention so much on the hate
Lost is the value of the souls at stake

Yours if not careful how you judge and rub
Forgotten the grace granted distributed in love
We're missing the point with each finger
He draws us in if we'd just linger

Long enough to see the opportunity
To cherish the bond made through our unity
Looking for love straight or gay
Missing the climax too late to penetrate

Once you decide you're friend or foe
The sunk opportunity to get to know
The Samaritan or stranger see if you knew
Depart from me now I warned you in Matthew

Week 50 - Oh Bride
by Sheila Ford

Oh Bride, Oh Bride make yourself clean
The Groom is to come, the word was forseen

Your garments are torn, your feet are uncovered
You have cleaved to your mom, and have slept with your
brother

Your hair has been cut, your lips are cracked
Your breast bear no fulfillment, they do lack

Who of him would desire, for your womb is barren
All adulterous suitors you allow to share in

Purify yourself oh' bride word yourself and be clean
The Bridegroom is to come, His coming was forseen

The engagement will soon be over, preparations are to pass
Left and called for the invite, will soon be cast

Oh bride, you must get ready, why look up into the sky
Your garments to be changed, the last days draw nigh

Week 51 - I'm Cold
by Sheila Ford

I'm sitting standing moving no matter where I go
I see people existing being but I don't want to know
We pass each other by nor do we try
To give a hand felt need denied

She's hurt he's sick they have no place to live
What I have is for me not extra could I give
Keep you distant please don't get too close
My emotional cup is lower than most

I desire to reach out my arm is frigid and cold
Numb by this culture not expected or told
Why am I blocking stopping substance I'm like ice
Interest to change I've heard it more than twice

Once years ago someone mentioned it in passing
That I could make a difference simply without asking
Much from me but basic in what I am
A living soul directed by greater than mere man

I feel the fire it warms me up
There is a deposit filling my cup
To overflow dispense at will
With tiny offerings He does fulfill
I feel the fire burning to the core
What I give out flows from who I adore

Week 52 - Where love goes
by Sheila Ford

I can feel you in my senses everything I hope to be
My dream my aspiration I lay them at your feet

There's so much I want to tell then there's more
I'm overwhelmed with emotion so much to explore

Where are the promises I want to see but don't want to look
Evident in a master plan I see them in your book

What will I find what's to expect giving up the other I forsook
Beyond my selfishness a part of where I need to look

Imagine love from Him others melted into me
Overflowing running spilling out as I live and just be

Love is powerful full of active action
Love is gentle reserved for the compassion

Love is kind it doesn't get mad
Love is patient enough to wait even when you're sad

Love doesn't brag or talk about what it will do
Love doesn't remember when the error is on you

Love wants to pour pour out out all over the universe
Filling every heart mind expanding the needed purse

Love is able not a fable every man woman every child
It has no limitations reaching every crevice across every mile

Reflection questions

Week 1 - You're in my dream
Reflection questions:
1. What have you dreamed, envisioned or considered spiritually, professionally or emotionally?
2. Did the dream die or live?

Application – Are you willing to reenact this dream or vision?

Accountability – Who will you tell about your dream and/or potential next steps?

Week 2 - He Stole something from me
Reflection questions:
1. What childhood experience or adult event made you feel powerless?
2. What action did you take?
3. Who did you share this experience with?

Application
- If applicable, share this experience with the appropriate authorities.
- Pray for forgiveness for the person that offended you.
- Forgive and release yourself of any self blame you may have absorbed unjustifiably.
- Pray for strength to physically and/or emotionally put this behind you.

Accountability

- Share this experience with a mature friend for the purpose of discerning your course of action.

Week 3 - Her name was Rosanne
Reflection questions:
1. Has anyone ever touched you inappropriately?
2. Do you ever think about it?

Application & Accountability – Share with a friend your thoughts and if possible pray about purging these thoughts from your mind.

Week 4 – I said "No" – Create your own discussion questions

Week 5 - Eye Candy
Reflection question:
1. Do you desire to be sexually appealing to people?
2. Do you look at women or men with lustful thoughts?

Application – Learn to start controlling your thought life by considering what you are thinking.

Accountability – Tell a friend your thoughts and intentions over this next week.

Week 6 - Hold Me
Reflection questions:
- Do you ever think you are going crazy?

Application - What do you do to bring yourself back to a place of mental peace?

Accountability – Ask a friend or trusted associate ways or tools they use for mental stability.

Week 7 - Gay or straight
Reflection questions:
1. Are you in a homosexual relationship?
2. Are you more concerned about what other people think than what God thinks about you?
3. Do you know God loves you and desires to hold you?

Application – Would you be willing to put your natural sexual activities on hold temporarily to entertain a spiritual relationship with God?

Accountability – Ask your partner to allow you some time to consider this matter. Ask God to protect your heart and mind as you pursue your relationship with Him.

Week 8 - Don't you want me
Reflection questions:
1. Does man's opinion of you matter?
2. How much?

Application – See if you can go one week without thinking about your physical appearance.

Accountability – Ask a friend to pray for or help you think about other things.

Week 9 - My Hair

Reflection questions:
1. Are you putting too much attention on your hair?
2. Do you spend more time thinking about your hair than you do your spiritual growth?

Application – Don't style you hair today!! Just kidding!
Consider how much time you spend on your hair.
Allocate the same amount of time toward your spiritual development this week.

Accountability – Ask one of your friends to join the challenge with you.

Week 10 - Circle of gold
Reflection questions:
1. If you are single, how often are you consumed with thoughts of being married?
2. If you are married, how much pride do you place in being married?
3. If you are married and a Christian do you consider your relationship with God to be your first marriage?

Application – What will you do, if anything to change your perspective on marriage?

Accountability – Who are you willing to share these insights with?

Week 11 - My past lover
Reflection questions:
1. If single, have you previously been or are you currently sexually active?
2. If married, did you have sex before you were married?

3. How do you believe those sexual activities impacted you?

Application – If negatively impacted, share this with one younger person or peer that has the potential to make the same mistake you did.

Accountability – Tell someone what you are going to do – ask them to hold you accountable for your actions.

Week 12 - A Woman or a girl
Reflections questions:
1. What area of your life needs maturing?
2. Is there one thing, person or idea you need to give up in order to grow spiritually or emotionally?

Application - What one action will you take this week to implement this maturing process?

Accountability - Who will you tell about your proposed action item?

Week 13 - He's pursuing me
Reflection questions:
1. Is there something God wants from you?
2. If so, what is it?

Application – Are you willing to give in to His pursuit of you today?

Accountability – Is there another person that would pray for or meditate on this place of surrender for you.

Week 14 - A desire of a heart
Reflection questions
- What is the desire of your heart?

Week 15 - Intimacy
Reflection question
- Would you like to deepen your intimacy with God?

Application - Start today by setting aside some quiet time to develop your relationship.

Accountability -Tell one friend about your new love interest.

Week 16 - His smile
Reflection questions:
1. Do you believe God sees you?
2. Do you believe He loves you?

Application – Name three things you think He loves about you.

Accountability – Ask a friend to tell you three things they admire about you.

Week 17 - Let Me love you
Reflection questions:
1. Will you allow yourself to be loved by God?
2. Will you allow yourself to be loved by others?
3. Do you believe you have to see a loving relationship modeled before you can dispense it yourself?

Application – Prayerfully prepare to be loved this week....*expect it.*

Accountability – Ask a friend to remind you to tell them how you were loved this week.

Week 18 - I need to hear your voice
Reflection question:
- Are you struggling with knowing what to do spiritually?

Application & Accountability – Find someone you trust spiritually and discuss your challenges. Ask them to prayerfully consider your options.

Week 19 - Kiss me
Reflection questions:
1. Do you have a hidden pain?
2. Would you consider trusting God to help you with this hurt?

Application – Would you pray right now and ask God to help you?

Accountability – Tell someone if you can.

Week 20 - A Longing
Reflection questions:
1. What 2-3 longings resonate most with you?
2. Why?

Application:

What can you do to have the longing fulfilled?

Accountability:
Do you need help? If so, who will you discuss this with for support?

Week 21 - A Virgin
Reflection questions:
1. If you have had sexual relationships outside of marriage, would you like a second chance to become a virgin?
2. Are you willing to forgive yourself of sexual sin?

Application – Tell yourself you made a mistake and ask God to forgive you of your past.

Accountability – Confide in a friend of your interest to move forward in purity.

Week 22 - My Chambers
Reflection questions:
- Would you like to have a private chamber for intimacy with God?

Application – Select a room or space and identify it as your place to meet Him. Commit to spending some quiet time in prayer, meditation, inspirational reading, music or silence to develop your relationship.

Accountability – Let someone know you need prayer support.

Week 23 - Lay me down
Reflection questions:
1. What does it mean to enter into the "rest" of God?
2. How often do you give or lay down the anxieties of your life to God?

Application – Decide to allocate some time this week to rest.

Accountability – Ask one other person to rest this week too. Do a post check in to determine if you both accomplished your tasks.

Week 24 - Your Hand
Reflection question:
- What does this poem move you to reflect on?

Week 25 - Open Wide
Reflection questions:
1. Are you willing to surrender yourself to God's love?
2. If not, what would you let go of in order to begin a new level of trust in God?

Application – What will you do differently starting today to further open yourself up to God?

Accountability – What person or people will you ask to hold you accountable to your decisions and new actions?

Week 26 - Come Passion
Reflection questions:
1. What are you passionate about?
2. Are there areas of service to in the world you have dismissed or neglected?

Application – What is stopping you from moving forward?

Accountability - Who do you need to help you get going?

Week 27 - Wash Over My Soul
Reflection questions:
1. What areas of your life need to be renewed or refreshed?
2. How do you know this?

Application – Where are you willing to go to become renewed?

Accountability – What friend knows you are challenged in this area?

Week 28 - My Body
Reflection questions:
1. Are you His Bride or His whore?
2. Why?

Application – What can you address today to change or improve your character?

Accountability – Who else knows about your challenges?

Week 29 - I see you everywhere I look
Reflection questions:
- Can you list 10 things you are thankful for?

Application - Out of those 10 things, identify which ones you believe came from God.

Accountability – Tell someone you are just getting to know one of the things you listed. i.e. tell someone on the bus stop, it's a great day and you are thankful for feeling good today!

Week 30 - My Feet
Reflection questions:
1. What direction are you going physically?
2. What direction are you going spiritually?

Application – Identify the guide you are using to help navigate your course.

Accountability – Who have you told about your journey.

Week 31 - Who I am
Reflection questions:
1. Do you know who you are?
2. Do you know your life purpose?

Application – Write out five statements or affirming words that characterize who you are.

Accountability – Tell someone you trust what these statements are.

Week 32 – My Two Husbands – Create your own reflection questions.

Week 33 - May 3
Reflection question
- What are you producing?

Application – List it or them

Accountability – Ask someone to tell you what they think you are producing.

Week 34 - You love me....love me not
Reflection questions:
1. Have you ever questioned God's love for you?
2. If so, what were the circumstances?
3. Do you still question if He loves you?

Application – Can you identify five things God has done/is doing for you right now? *i.e. you are breathing, you can see and read this text etc...*

Accountability – Who will you tell about the wonderful things God has done for you?

Week 35 - Cr'eye's that lie within sin
Reflection questions:

1. Have you ever taken the time to be quiet and reflect on your life, pain or what brings you joy?
2. Is there anything that hinders you from meditative reflection or prayer?

Application - Take 5-10 minutes each day this week and quietly pray or meditate. Ask for more clarity of your feelings and/or things that may concern you deeply.

Accountability - Tell a friend your desire to spend quiet time this week. Check in with them at the end of the week for accountability and support of your goal.

Week 36 - The Morning After
Reflection questions:
1. Do you need to give up something that you know is sinful?
2. What is it…say it aloud?

Application & Accountability – Tell someone about this sin this week and ask for help.

Week 37 – Catch my tear – Create your own reflection questions.

Week 38 - Tomorrow or Today
Reflection question:
- Are you anxious about your dreams, vision or aspirations?

Application – How can you disciple yourself to become more fully present in today?

Accountability – Who could you have as your buddy or prayer partner as you tackle this matter?

Week 39 - Bring me more
Reflection question:
- What do you need more of to strengthen your spiritual life?

Application - What do you need less of - to provide you with more?

Accountability - Create or set a goal that you will follow for 21 days. Tell someone that would challenge you and hold you accountable.

Week 40 – Lasting Love – Create your own reflection questions.

Week 41 - Your coming back
Reflection questions:
1. Do you believe Jesus Christ is coming back for those who love Him?
2. Has our culture dulled your spiritual sensitivity and eternal perspective?

Application I – If you would like to accept Jesus Christ into your heart see Appendix A.

Application II – If you believe in Christ what are you doing daily to prepare for His return?

Accountability – What spiritual person is able to help you strengthen your faith muscles?

Week 42 - Abortion
Reflection questions:
1. Have you ever had an abortion?
2. If so, do you believe God can forgive you?
3. Are you able to forgive yourself?

Application – Forgive yourself today.

Accountability – Be courageous and tell some you trust.

Week 43 - The other woman
Reflection questions:
1. Are you in a relationship with someone that has another woman? *i.e. an actual woman, drugs etc*
2. If so, how does this make you feel?

Application – What will you do to improve your emotional health?

Accountability – Will you pray and ask God for help?

Week 44 - Intimidate
Reflection questions:

1. Are there women or men that intimidate you or make you uncomfortable?
2. What is it about them that make you uncomfortable?

Application – Could you possibly spend 5 – 10 minutes getting to know this person better?

Accountability – Tell someone you know who this person is and the date you plan to have a short conversation with them.

Week 45 - Dear Daddy
Reflection questions:
1. As a woman of color what pain do you carry?
2. If you are not a woman of color what pain do you carry?

Application – Use this or these questions for discussion with a group.

Accountability – Identify as a group what action steps could be taken to address this pain.

Week 46 - The skin I'm in
Reflection questions:
1. Do you feel judged based on the color of your skin?
2. How does this affect your behavior?

Application – What can you do to alter feelings about this?

Accountability – Find a friend to discuss this matter in a constructive way.

Week 47 - Celebrating Life

Reflection questions:
1. What one thing have you done to impact another person's life?
2. Are you willing to meet someone new to share a piece of your life story?

Application – What can you do this week to celebrate your living by impacting another life through an act of kindness or gracious service?

Accountability – Would you take another person with you?

Week 48 - he doesn't love you
Reflection questions:
1. Are you in love with someone that doesn't love you back?
2. Are you trying to get all your love from a human being?

Application & Accountability – Ask a close friend if your behavior or relationships have reoccurring cycles?

Week 49 - Straight or gay
Reflection question:
•   Are you more concerned about someone's sexual preference than the state of their soul?

Application – Repent and ask God to show you how to love unconditionally.

Accountability – What person have you discussed your anger about this that you can confess your new approach?

Week 50 - Oh Bride
Reflection questions:
1. Is the Church/Bride ready for Christ return?
2. If you believe He is returning what can you do to prepare?

Week 51 - I'm cold
Reflection questions:
1. Have you become numb to the pain of others?
2. Do you believe you don't have enough extra to give?
3. Did you throw any food away last week?

Application – Search your closet and cabinets for one thing you don't use or could live without that may possibly be given to someone in need.

Accountability – Ask a friend or neighbor to do the same thing.

Week 52 - Where loves goes
Reflection question:
- Are you able to give love?

Application – Dispense two random acts of love this week.

Accountability – Ask someone to hold you accountable for your proposed random acts. *Do not tell them exactly what you are going to do until you have completed the acts.*

Appendix A

<u>If accepting Jesus Christ as your personal Savior please repeat:</u>

**Heavenly Father, I know that I have sinned against you and that my
sins separate me from you. I am truly sorry. I now want to turn away**

from my past sinful life and turn to you for forgiveness. **Please forgive me, and help me avoid sinning again. I believe that your son, Jesus Christ, died for my sins, was resurrected from the dead, is alive, and hears my prayer. I invite Jesus to become the Lord of my life, to reign in my heart from this day forward. Please send your Holy Spirit to help me follow You, and to do Your will for the rest of my life. In Jesus' name I pray, Amen.**

Congratulations! This is an incredible step in your life. Please inform someone immediately of your confession and life change.

I advise you connect with others that believe as you do for your increased development, growth and prayer support.

I would love to celebrate this life change with you. Please email me any comments you may have at info@missiontomobilization.com

www.ingramcontent.com/pod-product-compliance
Lightning Source LLC
Chambersburg PA
CBHW021450240626
47154CB00005B/1789